CW00566826

Living in God'

THE M-SERIES IS a collection of short, accessible papers and articles from Micah Global, being developed in response to the need for clear, authoritative statements on key themes. They form a foundation of historical and current ideas that contribute to our understanding and practice of integral mission. They aim to promote reflection, dialogue, articulation and action on the major concepts and issues that move us towards transforming mission.

The M-series is an essential resource for practitioners, theologians, students, leaders, and teachers.

M-Series from im:press

Living in God's Story

Understanding the Bible's Grand Narrative

Mark Galpin

Published by

im:press

An imprint of Micah Global

ISBN: 978-1720840961

Printed and bound by Ingram Spark

Introduction

Have you ever tried to put together a piece of machinery without knowing what it was you were constructing? Or have you tried to do a jigsaw puzzle without knowing the picture you were trying to create?

Growing up in a Christian family I had the privilege of being familiar with many of the stories of the Bible from a young age, but more recently I realised that I had no idea how, or even if, the stories all fitted together. I didn't know what kind of machine the individual parts actually made, or the picture that the individual pieces of the puzzle were creating. I set myself the challenge of trying to get to grips with this over-arching biblical story.

The purpose of this booklet is to briefly outline the story of the Bible as a whole, in six stages, in order to provide a framework that helps us understand how the different books of the Bible, written by many different authors, do tell *one* story. To help us understand this story I have used a triangle model[1] which highlights:

- the main characters involved at each stage of the story
- the relationships between these characters
- the key concepts, themes (or person) that determine these relationships
- the key roles of the characters

Each stage has a summary diagram in the form of a triangle with God at the top – indicating that God is the main character (Character A) – since the Bible is his–story.

1 This model draws on Chris Wright's 'triangles' in his book Old Testament Ethics for the People of God (Intervarsity Press, 2004), but develops them in a number of ways.

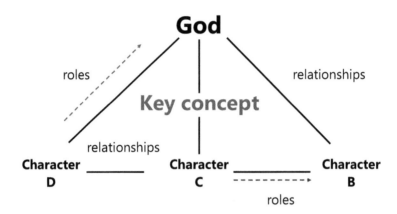

I have entitled this booklet Living in God's Story, because the Bible is the story of 'how the world came about, what went wrong, and what God has, is and will continue to do in order to set it right'.[2] It is the story of God's mission in the world (or the Missio Dei), a story in which we are called to live, and play an active role.

Why is this important?

Why is it important to understand this over-arching biblical story? Firstly, it helps us to understand how the different parts of the story fit together, so that as we read the Bible we can see how individual stories and books fit in with the rest of the biblical narrative. This helps our own understanding and deepens our engagement with God's word. This understanding also helps us interpret individual passages in the light of scripture as a whole, rather than taking them in isolation, and to see that the Gospel is 'constituted by the whole-Bible story of all that

2   This uses the language of Chris J. H. Wright in The Mission of God: Unlocking the Bible's Grand Narrative' (InterVarsity Press, 2006), and The Mission of God's People: A Biblical Theology of the Church's Mission (Zondervan, 2010). Both of these sources are drawn on heavily in this paper.

God both promised and accomplished and will bring to completion through Jesus of Nazareth, as promised Messiah, atoning Saviour and returning King.[3]

This biblical story or 'meta-narrative' also shapes our worldview – the fundamental assumptions that we make about the existence and nature of the world, God, time, and humanity. Our worldview impacts on how we perceive and understand the world and determines our values, attitudes, behaviour and culture as a whole. Growing in our understanding of the biblical worldview is fundamental if we are to be faithful in living out our lives as 'ambassadors' of Christ (2 Cor. 5:20) and to ensure we 'do not conform to the pattern of this world but (are) transformed by the renewing of (y)our mind(s)' (Romans 12:2). As followers of Christ we are to behave and think differently to the world around us – and developing a biblical worldview is essential to this.

> Knowing the biblical meta-narrative is essential if we are to understand the Gospel, live out the Gospel and present the Gospel faithfully to the world around us.

Chris Wright makes the point that 'without the biblical worldview, constituted by the biblical story, our understanding and presentation of the Gospel will be deficient.'[4] Often we have reduced and presented the Gospel as 'pie in the sky when we die', or simply a 'ticket to heaven' and therefore robbed it of its power and relevance to the world. In order to present the Gospel in all its power and relevancy, we need to present it as the biblical story.

In short, knowing the biblical meta-narrative is essential if we are to understand the Gospel, live out the Gospel and present the Gospel faithfully to the world around us.

3 Stott, J & Wright, C. Christian mission in the modern world (2015)
4 Ibid

The 6 stages of the Bible story

THE Bible consists of the Old and New Testaments, which are made up of a total of 66 books. Each of these books is divided up into chapters and verses, in order to help us find our way around the scriptures. However, for our purposes we are going to look at the bible in six parts as follows:

- Creation (Genesis 1 & 2)

- The Fall (Genesis 3)

- Covenant - the story of Israel (Genesis 12 to the end of the Old Testament)

- Christ - the life and ministry of Jesus including his death and resurrection

- Church - the present

- New Creation - the future – the new heavens and the new earth

We will end with a brief reflection on the implications for our role as the Church, and as individual Christians.

Creation (Genesis 1 & 2)

THE biblical story starts with the story of creation in Genesis 1 and 2. Genesis 1:1 reads, 'In the beginning God created the heavens and the earth'. From this very first verse we learn that God is the creator of all things in the heavens and on earth, and that he was there in the beginning. Nothing came before God. The created things are not divine in themselves and therefore should not be worshipped, but they were created by a divine God. God did not create the universe from parts of himself; the universe is separate from him, even if dependent on him. Nor did God create the world from already existing materials; nothing else but God existed before Creation.

God creates order and fills up the emptiness that was present prior to creation. He separates the light from the dark, sea from sky, and earth from water. He then fills up the heavens with the sun, moon, stars, planets and galaxies, and fills up the earth and sea with plants, birds, and fish. His evaluation of all this is that it is *'good'*.

On the sixth day, God creates the animals, and then humans. But there is a fundamental difference between the two. Humans are created in God's own image, animals are not. Although we are made from dust – we are made in God's image and this includes both Adam and Eve. Being made in the image of God includes our ability to reason, our moral conscience, our relational nature, and our creative ability. In 1:26 it is interesting to note that the language uses a plural form for God: "Let us make man in our image", emphasising that just as God lives in relationship with himself as the trinity, Father, Son and Holy Spirit, we are also made for relationship with him and with each other. Adam and

1. Creation (Genesis 1 & 2)

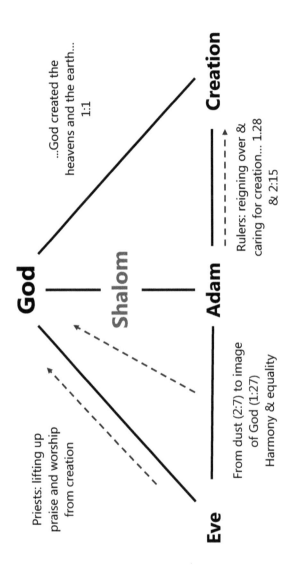

God

Shalom

Eve — **Adam** — - - - - ▸

Creation

...God created the heavens and the earth... 1:1

Rulers: reigning over & caring for creation... 1.28 & 2:15

From dust (2:7) to image of God (1:27) Harmony & equality

Priests: lifting up praise and worship from creation

God saw all that he had made and it was very good. 1:31

Eve, the first humans, are the parents of all humanity, and therefore all humans are equal, whatever their gender, race, ethnicity, caste, or socio-economic status.

We also learn that Adam and Eve were created to be one flesh and to do this they need to leave the custody of their parents and be joined together 'as one body' (2:24). God's intention is that this relationship was to be exclusive, between one man and one woman – not involving anyone else i.e. the relationship is to be monogamous. Sexual union between the man and his wife is both a sign and expression of this exclusive relationship. Adam and Eve were made to live in harmony and unity with each other.

At the end of the sixth day we are told that, 'God saw all that he had made and it was very good' (1:31). Creation as a whole, including the plants, birds, animals and humans, is judged to be very good by God.

What do we learn from this? We see that the whole of creation should be valued – as God judges it to be very good. The way we treat the whole of creation should reflect this value that God has placed on it, and the way that we treat others should reflect our understanding that they are made in God's image.

God blesses both the animals and birds (1:22) and Adam and Eve (1:28), and commands both to "Be fruitful and multiply; fill the earth" (1:22, 28). The green plants of the earth are given to all living things as food (1:29, 30).

Adam is placed in the garden and given the role to work it and take care of it (2:15), as both guardian and gardener, a role of active stewardship. Eve is made to be his companion and an equal partner in this (2:21). Adam's first task is the naming of the animals (2:19), indicating his authority over them. Note that creation was 'good' and then 'very good', but it was not perfect. Adam and Eve's role was both to protect and to build up creation, to develop it and to make it even better, using the creativity given to them by God.

> Adam and Eve's role was both to protect, and to build up creation... to make it even better, using the creativity given to them by God.

As the creator, God is the owner of all created things. Adam and Eve were delegated the role of servant kingship as God's representatives in the garden. This is the role that a good king should play in his kingdom – caring for everything and everyone they have authority over and responsibility for, rather than the exploitation that is characteristic of a bad ruler. As God's representatives Adam and Eve were also to live in close relationship with him and lift up praise and worship to him from the whole of creation - their role as priests. The Psalms make it clear that the overall purpose of creation is to give glory to God, and that the whole of creation lifts praise and glory to God (see Psalm 148 as an example).

We see that the garden is a place of order, fruitfulness, and harmony, i.e. shalom[5] – tended by Adam and Eve, and dwelt in by God. Sadly, the garden does not stay that way for very long, and in chapter 3 of Genesis we see that things start to go wrong.

---

5 *Shalom* is a complex Hebrew word incorporating the ideas of peace, justice and wellbeing with right relationships in all spheres of life.

Key concepts:

- God as a loving God who created the world and desires a relationship with us

- Creation / nature as good and very good but not divine

- Humanity made in God's image determining the equality and value (dignity) of all people

- As creator, God is the owner of all things. As an expression of love and obedience humanity takes care of all of God's creation

- The role of humanity to both protect and build up creation, and to live in relationship with God

The fall (Genesis 3)

When we look around the world we see the beauty of creation, but also that things have gone seriously wrong. Yes, we have 'filled the earth', but it is not the place of harmony and fruitfulness that God intended. So what happened?

Adam and Eve had been given complete freedom in the garden and could eat from any tree in the garden except for one: the tree of the knowledge of good and evil (2:17). But a serpent tempts Adam and Eve to disobey this one command[6]. This temptation involves both a distortion of God's word: "Did God really say..?" (3:1); as well as a denial of God's word: "You will not surely die?" (3:4). The temptation is that if they eat of the tree of knowledge they will 'become like God' (3:5) – knowing good and evil. Even though they are made in God's image, they are not satisfied with that, but want to become like God. Adam and Eve eat the fruit and through this act of disobedience they turn away from God and sin enters the garden.

This disobedience results in a fundamental change in nature of all aspects of creation – both humanity and the wider creation. The 'fall' corrupts the whole realm of nature and results in us being sinful from birth. Psalm 51:5 makes this clear. "Surely I was sinful at birth, sinful from the time my mother conceived me." It is not therefore that we are born sinless and that we have our own individual falls, but that from the time that sin entered the world through Adam and Eve's disobedience, the whole of creation, including humanity, is sinful by nature.

The impacts of the fall are multiple. Adam and Eve hide from God (3:8) because they are 'ashamed' of their nakedness (3:10). Their relationship with God is damaged and dominated by one of fear rather than free-

---

6 In Genesis 3:6 we are told that both Adam and Eve are present at the temptation (he 'was with her'!) and are therefore both to blame for this disobedience.

2. The Fall (Genesis 3)

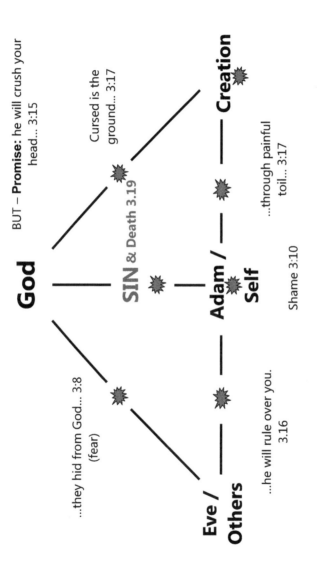

God

BUT – **Promise:** he will crush your head... 3:15

Cursed is the ground... 3:17

SIN & Death 3.19

Creation

Adam / Self

...through painful toil... 3:17

Shame 3:10

...they hid from God... 3:8 (fear)

Eve / Others

...he will rule over you. 3.16

dom and intimacy. In the past they probably ran to him to spend time with him, but now they hide from God.

Their nakedness is a source of shame for them, as they do not see themselves as people made in the image of God anymore. Their self-perception is therefore damaged, and shame enters the garden.

The relationship between Adam and Eve is also damaged. When asked by God what has happened, Adam blames both God and Eve ("The woman you put here with me, she gave me some fruit of the tree and I ate it." 3:12). This break of relationship is confirmed, and as a further consequence, Eve will be ruled over by her husband (3:16). This was not God's original intention, but a result of their disobedience.

> The fall and our ongoing disobedience have resulted in a 'holistic mess' – a corruption and distortion of the whole of creation... but within the mess of the fall there is a promise that gives hope.

Pain, toil and death enter the garden for the first time. Childbirth becomes a painful experience for Eve (3:16), and work becomes a burden for Adam since rather than being productive, the ground is cursed (3:17) and produces thorns and thistles.[7]

As humans we continue to 'curse the ground' through our actions, rather than caring for it as God originally intended. God also declares to Adam and Eve that they "will return to the ground from where you came for dust you are, and to dust you will return." (3:19) i.e. they will die. But within the tragedy God is compassionate and provides clothing for Adam and Eve (3:21). Finally, in their fallen state God declares that Adam and Eve should no longer have access to the 'tree of

---

7   A point developed by Dave Bookless in his book Planetwise: Dare to care for God's World (IVP, 2008)

life' (3:22), and so they are banished from the garden (3:23).

The 'fall' and our on-going disobedience have resulted in a 'holistic mess'[8] – a corruption and distortion of the whole of creation, including humanity. The impact of this fundamental change in nature was a disruption of all the relationships in the garden, the relationships between God and humanity, between Adam and Eve, between humanity and creation, and within creation itself. Adam and Eve's self-perception is also damaged through the fall. The world is no longer a place of harmony and fruitfulness (shalom), but one of fear, shame, enmity, pain, injustice, toil and death. We continue to see the impacts of the fall and our sinful nature in the world around us today, as we continue to act in sinful ways and fall short of the glory of God (Romans 3:23).

But within the 'mess' of the fall there is a promise that gives hope (3:15). The serpent who tempted Eve is cursed (3:14) and enmity is set up between the serpent and humans. But a promise is given that the 'offspring' of the woman will crush the head of the serpent i.e. will kill the serpent. "He will crush your head and you will strike his heel" (3:15). This indicates that one day a descendant of the woman, Eve, will be victorious over the serpent and all that it represents. This is seen as the first prophesy of Jesus' future victory over evil.

In the next few chapters of Genesis we see Cain and Abel (Chapter 4) – and the first murder case – a murder that tragically takes place between two brothers. In Chapters 6 to 9 we read the story of Noah and the flood. Noah is the one righteous man that God could find among all the people on earth, and so he is saved with his family and two of every living creature on earth. God cleanses the world by destroying the rest of humanity (who are not righteous) with a flood, but saves Noah and his family and the birds, animals and creatures that have come into the ark. In this we see God's concern and redemptive purpose for all of his creation. After the flood God blesses Noah and his sons and com-

8 A term used by Christopher J H Wright in The Mission of God (IVP, 2006)

mands them to be fruitful and fill the earth (9:1). A covenant is made between God and all the earth (9:13) that never again will there be a flood to destroy the earth (9:11). But even with the new start things continue to go wrong (9:20-23) and people continue to try to become like God, such as in the story of the Tower of Babel (Genesis 11).

Key concepts:

- Sin as disobedience and turning away from God

- The impact of sin in corrupting the whole of creation and resulting in a sinful nature, which leads to damaged relationships between God and humans, between humans themselves (including distorting the way humans see themselves), between humans and creation, and within creation as a whole

- Pain, death and suffering are a result of the fall

- The promise of a 'serpent crusher' descended from Eve who will eventually destroy the serpent and all it stands for

- The first covenant from God – not to destroy the world again

Covenant - The story of Israel, God's chosen people

Introduction

The third part of the biblical story starts with the call of Abraham (Genesis 12). This is the start of God's plan for the redemption of all of creation, of restoring the relationships damaged in the fall.

This part covers the rest of the Old Testament, from Genesis 12 to Malachi, which is the story of how God, or YHWH[9], engages with the nation of Israel within history. It is a long story covering approximately 2,000 years and makes up the majority of the Bible narrative. There are four key 'main characters' in this part of the story:

- God (the main character)
- The nation of Israel (of whom Abraham was the father)
- The land promised to Abraham and his descendants (the Promised Land)
- The nations other than Israel, known as the Gentiles

Here we will highlight just the key themes of this story, and how these different characters interact in the story. This is summarised in Diagram 3 below.

The call of Abraham – to 'go and be a blessing'

This part of the story starts with God calling Abraham out of the place where he is living to go to a place that God promises to show him - the

---

9 YHWH is the translation of the original Hebrew written name for the God of Israel, the name he used to introduce himself to Moses at the burning bush. It is commonly pronounced Yahweh. In the Bible this holy name is replaced with the LORD.

Promised Land. This command to 'go' is accompanied by a promise – that God will make Abraham into a great nation and that all peoples on earth will be blessed through him (12:2,3). God's choosing of Abraham, and through him the nation of Israel, is therefore not just to bless Abraham and the Israelites, but to bless all nations and all peoples on earth. The election of Israel (through Abraham) is therefore a great responsibility rather than an act of favouritism.

> God's choosing of Abraham, and through him the nation of Israel, is therefore not just to bless Abraham and the Israelites, but to bless all nations and all people on earth.

Abraham is obedient to this call and leaves behind his ancestral homeland, together with its traditional belief systems, and follows God. He is eventually blessed with a son Isaac, who goes on to bear Jacob who is renamed 'Israel' and from whom the nation of Israel gets its name. Jacob's 12 sons form the 12 tribes of the nation of Israel, including Joseph. Joseph's brothers are jealous of their father's favourite and sell Joseph into slavery in Egypt (Genesis 37).

The exodus

A key story in the Old Testament is the rescuing of the Israelites from captivity in Egypt. This is recorded in the book of Exodus.

After Joseph is sold into slavery in Egypt, the family of Jacob are forced to emigrate to Egypt due to the famine across the region. They are eventually reconciled with their brother Joseph, who is now second in command to Pharaoh, and has provided for them and many others through the years of famine, and also provides them with land to settle in Egypt.

However, over the next 400 years or so the memory of Joseph fades, and the Egyptians feel threatened by the growing numbers of Israelites living amongst them, and so they are put into slavery. In their suffering, they cry out to God, and God calls Moses to lead his people out of slavery.

There follows a powerful encounter between Pharaoh and YHWH: plagues of blood, frogs, gnats, flies, livestock disease, boils, hail, locusts and darkness. These culminate in the death of the firstborn in all Egyptian families – but the Israelites escape this as they have obediently made the sacrifice of a lamb and put the blood of the lamb onto the doorposts of their houses, so the angel of death passes over them (the Pass-over). This points toward the sacrifice of Christ for the redemption of all.

This final plague leads to the Israelites' release from Egypt – though the Egyptians then chase the Israelites, but drown when crossing the waters that God had held back for the Israelites.

Here we see God's love and compassion for his people, his hatred of the injustice perpetrated against them, and his concern for all aspects of his people's lives. Slavery under the Egyptians was spiritual, political and socio-economic. They did not have freedom to worship YHWH, they were spiritual slaves. But in addition they were slaves politically and socially – without the power to determine their own leaders and future. They were slaves economically as they worked for their captors rather than themselves[10].

> Through the exodus... we see God's love and compassion for his people, his hatred of the injustice perpetrated against them, and his concern for all aspects of his people's lives.

10 Wright C. J. H. The mission of God: Unlocking the Bible's Grand Narrative (2016)

God brings the Israelites out of Egypt and frees them from all these aspects of bondage – spiritual, political, social and economic. The exodus is a story of holistic liberation and demonstrates clearly that YHWH was not only God of the Israelites, but also the God who has power and authority over all creation and all empires – including Egypt[11].

The law

After the Israelites are liberated from Egypt, God confirms his covenant (originally made with Abraham) at Mount Sinai (Exodus 19:5) and introduces the law. The law is put in place to guide the nation of Israel in all aspects of life, to ensure that through obedience to it they live in a way that is glorifying to God – and are a light and blessing to 'all the nations' (see Diagram 3 below). Central to the law are the Ten Commandments (Exodus 20:1 – 17). The books of Leviticus, Numbers and Deuteronomy focus on the law.

The law governs the relationships between the Israelites and YHWH i.e. spiritual issues, primarily through the system of sacrifice, to ensure their righteousness before God (e.g. Leviticus 6). Righteousness refers to their 'right-ness' and is closely related to just-ness or justice. The tabernacle, then later the temple, is the dwelling place of God among the people (the point at which heaven and earth meet), where people come to worship him. But God is separated from his people, as a righteous, holy God cannot live among a sinful

> The law is put in place to guide the nation of Israel in all aspects of life, to ensure that through obedience to it they live in a way that is glorifying to God – and are a light and blessing to 'all the nations'.

11 ibid

people. Only the high priests can enter the most Holy Place where God resides, and only after extensive purification rites. The temple is however a pointer and example of God's intention – a place where he dwells amongst his people and his people come to worship him.

The law also included rules as to how the nation of Israel was to function as a 'model' society. This covered socio-economic issues to ensure that society was just and fair and that extremes of poverty and wealth did not occur. The Jubilee laws (Leviticus 25) ensured that every so often the inequalities in society that would inevitably arise were evened out once more, and property was returned to its original owners. Laws also stipulated the care of and provision for widows, orphans and aliens – the poor and marginalised of society (Deuteronomy 24:18-22).

Other laws covered how the Israelites were to treat the land. These include the seventh year of rest for the land (Leviticus 25); and sustainable harvesting of natural wildlife[12] (Deut 22:6). The Israelites were to be a model to other nations. The law emphasised that the earth (and therefore the land) belongs to God and human beings are only tenants on it, not owners. The Psalms reiterate this, such as in Psalm 24:1, 'The Earth is the Lord's and everything in it.'

> The law ... covered spiritual, socio-economic, political and environmental issues, and reflected God's character, a God of love and justice who is concerned with all aspects of his people's lives.

Other laws dealt with the relationship the nation of Israel should have with other nations, emphasising the need to be separate and distinct and not get involved with their religious beliefs and practices (Deuteronomy 7:1-6, 26:19).

12 Bookless, D. Planetwise. 2008

The law covered spiritual, socio-economic, political and environmental issues, and reflected God's character, a God of love and justice who is concerned with all aspects of his people's lives and the whole of creation.

Conquest

After wandering in the desert for 40 years due to their disobedience, God brings the people of Israel to the edge of the Promised Land, and under the leadership of Joshua, they cross over the River Jordan (see the book of Joshua). God then helps the Israelites to conquer the tribes currently occupying the land promised to them. When they are obedient to God they are successful (e.g. Jericho), but when they are disobedient they are defeated (e.g. Ai). Gradually the other tribes are defeated and the Israelites take over the land and settle within it.

Judges then kings

One of the unique aspects of the nation of Israel was that they were not to have a king like other nations, as YHWH was their king. They were therefore led by a number of judges (see the book of Judges for the stories about them) who God raised up to deliver them from their oppressors. But the people always returned to their evil ways and worshipped other gods, incurring God's wrath and discipline for their disobedience and unfaithfulness, before once again repenting and being delivered by the Lord (see Judges 2:16-23). A cycle of disobedience, punishment and repentance characterised this period in Israel's history.

However, the people of Israel decided that they wanted to be like other nations and have a king (see 1 Samuel 8). God, through the prophet Samuel, warns them against this, but the people get their way and Saul is made king followed by David, then Solomon, and then a succession of other kings through history, most of whom paid little attention to God or the law.

During Solomon's reign the temple is built, and Israel becomes a nation

3. Covenant

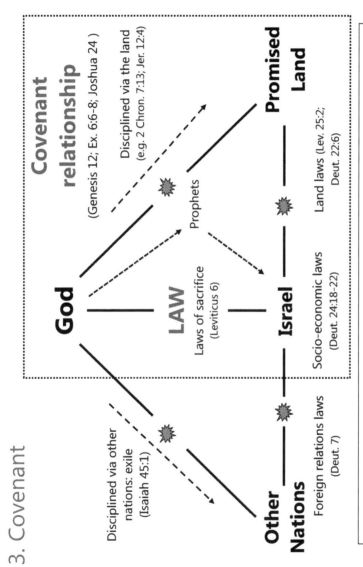

Covenant relationship
(Genesis 12; Ex. 6:6-8; Joshua 24)

Disciplined via the land
(e.g. 2 Chron. 7:13; Jer. 12:4)

God

LAW

Laws of sacrifice
(Leviticus 6)

Prophets

Promised Land

Land laws (Lev. 25:2;
Deut. 22:6)

Israel

Socio-economic laws
(Deut. 24:18-22)

Disciplined via other
nations: exile
(Isaiah 45:1)

Other Nations

Foreign relations laws
(Deut. 7)

Key stages of the OT story

Patriarchs – Exodus – Conquest – Judges – United kingdom – Divided kingdom – Exile – Return

that is respected and revered across the known world. However, due to the exploitation of the people, the northern tribes become disgruntled. When Solomon's son Rehoboam takes over as king he is even more exploitative than his father (1 Kings 12) and the ten tribes in the north rebel against him. There is a brief civil war and the nation of Israel is split into two, Israel in the north and Judah to the south.

Prophets – guardians of the covenant

Unfortunately, the people of Israel were not faithful and did not keep the law. At times, depending on the character of their ruler, they did better than other times, but often, rather than being a light and blessing to the nations and drawing them into relationship with YHWH, they brought shame on the God they professed to follow.

Key books of the prophets include Isaiah, Jeremiah, and Ezekiel, as well as the many 'minor' prophets (Amos, Joel, Micah, Zechariah etc.). The prophets acted as spokespersons for God, speaking into the situation and highlighting the disobedience of the people and warning them of the consequences of their disobedience. However, the prophets also reminded them of the covenant relationship they had with God and pointed toward the future with hope.

This covenant relationship did not mean that the Israelites would avoid the consequences of their sinfulness. God, being loving and just, disciplines the Israelites for their disobedience, in order to bring them back to him. Two key areas of disobedience are emphasised – idolatry i.e. the worship of other gods (e.g. Isaiah 44:6-23; Ezekiel 8), and social injustice (e.g. Isaiah 58; Jeremiah 22:13-17; Ezekiel 16:49).

> "Woe to those who make unjust laws, to those who issue oppressive decrees, to deprive the poor of their rights and withhold justice from the oppressed of my people, making widows their prey and robbing the fatherless." Isaiah 10:1,2

These two are related; as the Israelites turn away from worshipping the God of love and justice they fail to act with love and justice.

God uses two key mechanisms for disciplining Israel for their disobedience (see Diagram 3). Firstly, they are disciplined through the land, for example by drought and natural disasters (2 Chronicles 7:13; Jeremiah 12:4). This shows God's sovereignty over all of creation.

Secondly, God uses the nations surrounding Israel to discipline the Israelites for their unfaithfulness. This demonstrates that God is not just God over Israel, but also God over other nations, and uses them to bring about his purposes (Isaiah 45:1), even though they do not follow him.

> The prophets spoke of God's judgment but also looked forward with hope, to a time when the nation of Israel would be restored and would become a blessing to all nations, as promised to Abraham.

After the kingdom is divided, the northern kingdom lasts for about 200 years and is ruled over by a succession of kings, none of whom were faithful to God. God has finally had enough and they are attacked and taken into exile by the Assyrians. The Southern Kingdom of Judah lasts 136 years longer with about 8 of its 20 kings being faithful to God, for at least some of their reign. However, eventually they too are attacked, the city of Jerusalem and the temple is destroyed, and the people are taken into exile by the Babylonians (2 Kings 25). This story is also told in 2 Chronicles 36 and by Jeremiah (Jeremiah 39), and the emotional shock and loss of these events is described by Jeremiah in the book of Lamentations.

Restoration and hope

The prophets spoke of God's judgment, but also looked forward with hope, to a time when the nation of Israel would be restored and would become a blessing to all nations, as promised to Abraham. As we look back over the story we can see that three key events were looked forward to by the prophets and the people of Israel.

> The story of the nation of Israel... the story of God's continued faithfulness to the people of Israel, despite their repeated unfaithfulness to him.

The first of these events was the return and restoration of Israel after the exile (Ezekiel 37:21,22; Jeremiah 33). The second event was the coming of the Messiah or the Christ (Isaiah 53), who would take onto himself the sins of all people as the ultimate atoning sacrifice. The third event predicted by the prophets is the final stage of the story – when Christ will return once again, and the new heavens and the new earth will be established for ever and ever (Isaiah 65:17 ff). Although the prophets themselves could not see these as three distinct events occurring in this order, as we look back to their teachings and the first two of these events which have occurred, we can see them in this way.

At the end of the Old Testament the Persians defeat the Babylonians who are holding the Israelites in exile. Through the testimony of Daniel, God uses Cyrus the King of Persia to release the Israelites. After 70 years in exile, the Israelites are allowed to return to the land they had lived in, the Promised Land. The city of Jerusalem and the temple are rebuilt (see the books of Ezra and Nehemiah) as the prophets had predicted, but never attain their former glory. The nation of Israel remains a small province surrounded by and often ruled by foreign powers. However, never again did the people of Israel turn to idolatry and worship other gods. And so the Israelites waited for the time when all that the prophets had promised would come to pass.

This third part of the Bible story, the story of the nation of Israel, can be summarised as the story of God's continued faithfulness to the people of Israel, despite their repeated unfaithfulness to him.

Key points:

- God's plan to use Israel to be 'a blessing to all nations' and to draw all nations into relationship with Him

- God's love and justice seen through the redeeming of his people through the 'holistic liberation' of the exodus

- YHWH as God over all peoples and nations and all of creation

- The law as God's instructions to Israel, reflecting God's character of love and justice and his concern for all of his creation, to ensure they were a light and blessing to the nations

- The role of the prophets as God's spokespersons, highlighting to Israel their idolatry and injustice, calling them back to relationship with YHWH, and looking forward to the future with hope

- God's compassion and faithfulness in forgiving Israel and bringing them back into relationship with him, despite their repeated unfaithfulness

Jesus Christ – The messiah

THROUGHOUT the story of the Old Testament, starting with Genesis 3:15, we see that God has a plan to redeem creation once more, and bring it back into relationship with him. The Old Testament prophets clearly indicate that a messiah will come and bring about this final redemptive act, and that through this, the promised blessing to all nations from Abraham's seed and David's line would be fulfilled.

The next stage is the story of Jesus Christ, the messiah, the climactic episode in God's plan of redemption and the story of his redemptive work in human history[13].

Birth – the promised messiah

The New Testament starts with outlining the genealogy or ancestry of Jesus (Matthew 1:1-17). This clearly establishes that Jesus is the messiah prophesied in the Old Testament, the one from David's line and Abraham's seed. Luke traces Jesus' ancestry back to Adam (Luke 3:21-38), demonstrating that Jesus is the 'serpent crusher' prophesied in Genesis 3:15.

Jesus is born as a helpless baby, into squalor and relative poverty (in a cow-shed), to relatively poor parents, far away even from his own home and centres of power. These events were prophesied by the prophet Isaiah 700 years earlier (Isaiah 7, 9, 11). His birth is miraculous, as his mother Mary is a virgin, who conceives by the power of the Holy Spirit (Matthew 1:18-22). His birth is heralded by a star in the sky, and angels in the heavens who proclaim to outcast shepherds that the long-awaited messiah has been born (Luke 2:10,11). He is visited by these shepherds and also by wise men from the east who give him gifts that reflect: his his kingship (gold), his holiness (frankincense), his

13 Bartholomew & Goheen, The Drama of Scripture. (2006).

future death (myrrh) Matthew 2.

Herod, the local ruler, is threatened by this new king he has heard about and, in an attempt to get rid of him, he commits genocide by killing all the baby boys under a certain age in the area. However, Jesus' parents escape, becoming refugees in Egypt. Later when Jesus returns he spends the rest of his childhood and early adulthood in the home of his earthly father in Nazareth, working with him as a carpenter.

Start of Jesus' ministry – revealed Lord

Jesus starts his ministry when he is about 30 years old. In the months prior to this John the Baptist had been preaching in the desert, calling the people to repentance, baptising them, and prophesying the coming of the messiah (Luke 3). John also baptises Jesus at his request, and the Holy Spirit descends upon him and a voice from Heaven declares, "You are my Son whom I love; with you I am well pleased." (Luke 3.22).

Jesus goes on to be tempted in the desert for 40 days and then starts teaching in the synagogues throughout Galilee. He then goes to the synagogue in Nazareth, his home town, and reads out the passage of scripture from the prophet Isaiah.

> "The Spirit of the Lord is upon me, for he has anointed me to preach good news to the poor. He has sent me to proclaim freedom for the prisoners and recovery of sight for the blind, to release the oppressed and proclaim the year of the Lord's favour." (Luke 4: 14-21)

As Jesus sits down he clearly states that in him this scripture is fulfilled (Luke 4:21), thereby claiming to be the saviour prophesied by Isaiah and clearly indicating the nature of his ministry.

The proclamation and demonstration of the kingdom

His ministry does indeed fulfill this mission, as he preaches the good news, heals the sick, casts out demons, feeds the hungry, restores dignity to those who feel shame, gives hope to the hopeless, and challenges the rich and the powerful.

His teaching focuses on the nature of the 'kingdom' that he has come to establish. We learn that the kingdom is immensely valuable and worth giving everything up for (stories of the pearl and treasure, Matthew 13:44,45), that it is growing (the stories of the yeast and mustard seed, Matthew 13:31-35), and that it is mixed up and difficult to separate from the kingdom of this world – and that will only happen at the final judgment (the story of the weeds in the field, Matthew 13:24-30, 36-43).

> He declares not a revolution of violence to overthrow the Roman authorities (as hoped and expected by many), but a revolution of love and justice.

The ethics of the kingdom are also clearly explained in Jesus' teaching in the Sermon on the Mount (Matthew 5 to 7). This is summarised in the beatitudes, where Jesus proclaims blessing on those that are poor, those who mourn, the meek, those who thirst for righteousness, the merciful, the pure in heart, the peacemakers, and those who are persecuted (Matthew 5:3-12; Luke 6:20-26), groups who are far from blessed in normal society.

In Matthew the beatitudes are followed by Jesus' challenge to be salt and light in the world (Matthew 5:13-16) and to cause others to give praise to God because of the good deeds they see in our lives.

The kingdom that Jesus declares and demonstrates is one in which the values of the world are turned upside down, and the last become first. He declares not a revolution of violence to overthrow the Roman authorities (as hoped and expected by many), but a revolution of love and justice. The kingdom is demonstrated not only in his teaching, but also in his life. He breaks down traditional hierarchies and barriers of poverty, caste, and gender, and demonstrates his love for all people (e.g. in his interaction with the Samaritan woman, John 4). Jesus demonstrates the kingdom through signs, words and deeds. He is in close fellowship with his heavenly father, regularly spending time in prayer, and is empowered and sustained by the power of the Holy Spirit.

The beginning of the kingdom community

Early on in his ministry in Galilee, Jesus begins to form a community around him from those who respond to his message, repent and put their faith in him. Some are called to remain in their homes as part of that kingdom community; others are called to follow him as his disciples[14] (John 1). Twelve disciples are designated as 'apostles', representing the 12 tribes of Israel. These twelve are appointed to be 'with him, and that he might send them out to preach, and to have authority to drive out demons' (Mark 3:13-19). Later on we see that the twelve are sent out to teach from village to village, calling people to repent, driving out demons and anointing the sick with oil (Mark 6:6-12). Through their ministry many people are healed and freed from demon possession.

> **Jesus begins to form a community around him from those who respond to his message, repent and put their faith in him.**

For the first two years Jesus' ministry focuses on the area of Galilee, but he then journeys outside Galilee to Gentile territory, and continues to teach and minister, while preparing his disciples to carry on his work.[15]

14 Bartholomew & Goheen. The Drama of Scripture. (2006)
15 Ibid

Jesus' radical message and demonstration of a new kingdom attracts the powerless and the needy, those who recognise their weakness and needs - those who are least in the kingdoms of the world. However, his teaching and ministry are seen as a threat to those in power, particularly by the religious authorities, whom he openly criticises (Luke 11: 37-53). His confrontation of the authorities comes to a climax with his triumphal entry into Jerusalem (Matthew 21:1-11; Luke 19:28 ff) and his righteous anger in the temple as he turns over the tables and drives out the money changers from the court of the gentiles for their corrupt practices (Matthew 11:12-17).

Death and resurrection – victory of the kingdom

The religious leaders plot his capture. Bribing one of his disciples to betray him they come with armed guards to arrest him. Jesus is arrested and then mocked and beaten before being taken before the council of Jewish elders, and then on to Pilate and Herod. Pilate gives in to the demands of the crowd and hands Jesus over for crucifixion. He is led out of the city, nailed to a cross and left to die.

Even though Jesus predicted that this would happen and explained to his disciples that it must happen, they are shocked and dismayed, and scatter. It appears that the final battle between the kingdom of God and the powers of evil has been lost, when in fact through the cross 'God delivers the final death blow to human sin and rebellion and accomplishes the salvation of this world.'[16]

Three days later some women go to the tomb where Jesus' body is buried. They find it empty and hurry back to tell the disciples. Jesus then appears to the disciples and others – having risen from the dead, as he said he would. After several days with them he returns to his father in heaven, having completed the work he came to do on earth (see John 17:4; Phil. 2: 1-11).

16 Ibid

What is the meaning of this? Paul's writings clearly show us that, Christ through his death and resurrection achieved, what the law failed to do:

> "For what the law was powerless to do..., God did by sending his own Son... to be a sin offering." (Romans 8:3)

Due to humankind's sinful nature, the Law could not achieve what it set out to do. A new covenant was needed, and a new and final sacrifice to seal that covenant, which promises salvation once and for all, for everyone.

> "Christ is the mediator of a new covenant..., the promised eternal inheritance." (Hebrews 9:15)

Through this sacrifice Jesus took our sins, and the punishment for these, onto himself. In doing this he takes away our sinful nature and makes it possible for us to appear before God as righteous (Romans 5:19). Therefore, if we confess our sins and put our faith in Jesus Christ, he forgives us our sins (1 John 2:2) and restores us to relationship with him. The relationship between man and God broken initially at the fall, is therefore restored through Christ, and through his blood we who are in Christ are reconciled to God (2 Corinthians 5:18; Colossians 1:19,20). The Gospels and Paul's writing also give us other 'pictures' to help us understand this. Jesus himself says:

> "...the Son of Man (Jesus) did not come to be served, but to serve, and to give his life as a ransom for many." (Matthew 20:28; Mark 10:45)

From this we understand that Jesus' death was like a ransom payment, paid to release us from sin and eternal death. Through his resurrection, sin and death are conquered, and we are released from the bondage of sin and the curse of death (Romans 6:22,23; Colossians 2:15; 2 Timothy 1:10).

However, it is not just the relationship between humanity and God that is restored through Jesus. Paul affirms that through Christ all created things are reconciled (Ephesians 1:10; Colossians 1:15-20). In Ephesians we read that the relationships between Jews and Gentiles, men and women, slave and free are restored and all become one in Christ Jesus (Ephesians 2: 14-18). The damaged relationship between different parts of humanity (which started between Adam and Eve at the fall), are therefore also restored through Christ.

> Through Jesus we see the pinnacle and cosmic nature of God's redemptive plan to once more reconcile all things to himself

The result of the change from our sinful nature and the restoration of these relationships is that we are now released to fulfill the roles God gave us initially in the garden. Romans 8 describes creation as 'wait(ing) in eager expectation for the children of God to be revealed' (Romans 8:19), and being 'liberated from its bondage to decay' (Romans 8:21) as through Christ we take on our role as his sons and daughters – as 'servant kings' stewarding creation, and as priests lifting up praise and worship to him.

Through Jesus we see the pinnacle and the cosmic nature of God's redemptive plan. In Colossians 1:15-20, we read that Jesus is fully God, and that he is the agent, the purpose, the sustainer and the redeemer of all creation, and through his death on the cross he has made peace and reconciled to himself all things.

4. Christ

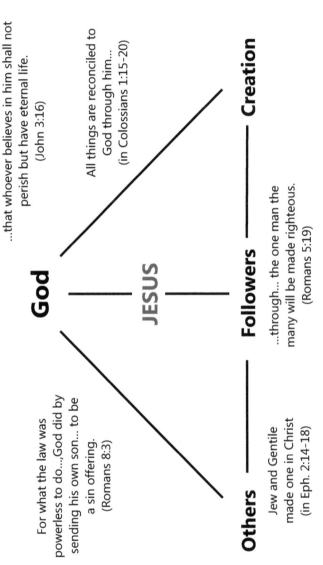

God

..that whoever believes in him shall not perish but have eternal life.
(John 3:16)

All things are reconciled to God through him...
(in Colossians 1:15-20)

For what the law was powerless to do...God did by sending his own son... to be a sin offering.
(Romans 8:3)

JESUS

Creation

Followers

..through... the one man the many will be made righteous.
(Romans 5:19)

Others

Jew and Gentile made one in Christ
(in Eph. 2:14-18)

Christ is the mediator of a new covenant... the promised eternal inheritance (Hebrews 9:15)

Key points:

- Jesus as the promised messiah, prophesied throughout the Old Testament (from Genesis 3:15 onwards)

- Jesus' incarnation as a human being, and his life and teachings that demonstrate his kingdom of love and justice

- Jesus' death and crucifixion as the 'penalty' and 'ransom payment' for the sins of the whole world; and the sacrifice to seal a new and final covenant for all people, and to establish his kingdom

- By confessing our sins and putting our faith in Jesus we are forgiven our sins and appear righteous before God, joining his kingdom

- Jesus' resurrection as the final victory over death and sin

- Our freedom in Christ to fulfill the roles of 'priests' and 'servant kings' / 'stewards' given to us at creation, as members of his kingdom

- The cosmic nature of God's redemptive plan through Jesus who reconciles all things and redeems the whole of creation

Church – The kingdom community

THE book of the Acts of the Apostles records the next part of the story, the time between Jesus' life on earth and his final return. After Jesus' ascension to heaven the apostles return to Jerusalem (Acts 1:1-12). As they gather to celebrate the Feast of Weeks they are filled with the Holy Spirit and begin to speak in many different languages. Through their preaching and many signs and wonders, the fellowship of believers grows rapidly. They form a radical community, sharing their possessions, caring for the poor, and testifying to the resurrection of Jesus (Acts 4:32 – 35). In this way, they lived in radical contrast to society around them, and gave witness to Christ through their words, their deeds and the whole of their lives.

However, opposition arises and the church is persecuted and scattered (Acts 8), and in this way the Gospel is spread from Jerusalem to Samaria and then to the ends of the earth. The rest of the book of Acts records the spread of the Gospel and the growth of the church, initially through Peter's leadership and then through Paul's missionary journeys.

We are living in this part of the story, the time between Christ's life on earth and his return - between the inauguration of his kingdom and the fulfillment of that kingdom in the future. What are the implications of that for our lives as individuals and as a church?

In 2 Corinthians 5, Paul calls us to live as 'ambassadors' of Christ, representing him in the world. This is both a great privilege as well as a great responsibility, as others will judge Christ from what they see in our lives. In 2 Peter 3:13 we are challenged to live in expectation of the fulfillment of his kingdom.

We are called to offer our bodies as living sacrifices, to be different to the world around us, to 'be transformed' by the renewing of our minds. (Romans 12:1,2)

The church, and all followers of Christ therefore stand in continuity with the Israelites who were tasked to be distinct and separate in the way they lived, but fully engaged, and a blessing to all those around them. We have been 'called out' to take responsibility for the world around us[17]. But we cannot do that in our own strength, therefore when Christ ascended to heaven he sent the Holy Spirit as a counselor, who empowers and strengthens us to live as members of his kingdom, within this world. The Holy Spirit gives us gifts to exercise in this role (Rom 12: 6-8), and the fruits of the Spirit (Galatians 5: 22,23) should be clearly seen in our lives.

> (We)...therefore stand in continuity with the Israelites who were tasked to be distinct and separate in the way they lived, but engaged and a blessing to all those around them.

Our example is both that of Jesus himself (1 John 2:6; 1 Peter 2:21), as well as the early church, demonstrating God's kingdom through every aspect of our lives.

As members of the church we therefore live with the tension of knowing that God's kingdom has been inaugurated, and we are called to live as members of that kingdom, but also that it is not yet fully established and will only be fulfilled completely when Christ returns.

17 Reimer, J. Missio Politica. (2017)

5. The Church (now)

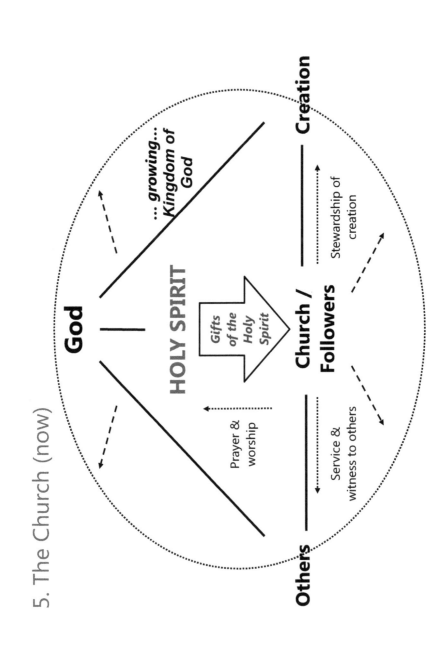

As a church and as individuals we can summarise our role as being in three key areas of activity (see diagram 5):

- Worship of and prayer to God

- Sharing the good news by practically demonstrating God's love and verbally sharing the Gospel with others (service and witness), particularly the poor and victims of injustice

- And through the building up and care of creation (stewardship)

Key points:

- God's reign as his 'kingdom here on earth', which has begun but has not yet been completed

- The nature of God's kingdom as a kingdom of love and justice, where the last shall come first

- Our identity as 'ambassadors' of Christ, both representing and building his kingdom here on earth

- Our roles of lifting praise and worship to him, serving and witnessing to others, and stewarding creation

- The Holy Spirit as a helper and companion to equip and empower us to carry out these roles

New Creation - The fulfillment of the kingdom

B OTH the prophets of the Old Testament and the Revelation of John (the last book of the Bible), look forward to give us a picture of the final stage of history. When Christ comes again, the new kingdom that he started when he came to earth will be brought to completion, and will continue for ever and ever (Revelation 11:15) and all the relationships broken at the fall will be fully restored (see Diagram 6). The picture we are given has elements of the city of Jerusalem, the temple, and the garden of Eden. This is called the 'new heavens and new earth', and contains the 'new Jerusalem'.

A key passage describing this is Revelation 21:1-4

> "Then I saw a new heaven and a new earth, for the first heaven and the first earth had passed away, and there was no longer any sea. I saw the Holy City, the New Jerusalem, coming down out of heaven from God, prepared as a bride beautifully dressed for her husband. And I heard a loud voice from the throne saying, "Now the dwelling of God is with men, and he will live with them. They will be his people and God himself will be with them and be their God. He will wipe every tear from their eyes. There will be no more death or mourning or crying or pain, for the old order of things has passed away.""

So what are these 'new heavens and new earth' and 'new Jerusalem' like?

It is a beautiful city made of gold and precious gems (Revelation 21:18-21), big enough to contain all the children of God and occupied by people from every nation (Revelation 21:26).

God dwells in the city with its inhabitants (Revelation 21:3) – just as he did in the garden before the fall. There is no need for a temple, or the sun, as his glory provides the light for the city. There is no more death or crying, or mourning or weeping (Revelation 21:4). Harmony is restored in all of creation – even the lion and the lamb lie down together (Isaiah 65 and 11:6-9).

> When we sin we harm ourselves, the people around us, the wider community and society we are part of, and the environment we live in - all things that God loves.

The curse placed on creation through the fall is lifted (Revelation 22:3), and creation is liberated from decay – as we take up our rightful and God-intended roles as 'servant kings', reigning over creation (Romans 8:19-24; Revelation 22:5). In addition, access to the tree of life which was cut off after the fall is now restored, and the leaves of the trees are used for the healing of the nations (Revelation 22:2). Shalom is once again restored.

This is the reason for the hope that we have as Christians. While currently we live with the tension of the 'now and not yet' of the kingdom, we know that eventually God's kingdom will be fully established and last for ever and ever. That is what we are working and looking forward to as God's kingdom community.

Sometimes as Christians we are overly focused on heaven. However, heaven is not our final destination, it is just the resting place where we go when we die to await the final resurrection and the fulfillment of God's kingdom in the new heavens and the new earth[18].

When we sin we harm ourselves, the people around us, the wider community and society we are part of, and the environment we live in – all

---

18 See Wright, Tom. Surprised by Hope (SPCK, 2007) for a full exploration of this.

6. New Creation

Others

Judged by Christ
Rev. 11:18

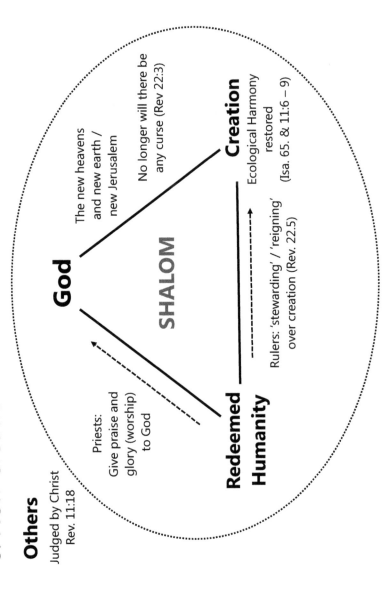

God

The new heavens
and new earth /
new Jerusalem

No longer will there be
any curse (Rev 22:3)

Creation

Ecological Harmony
restored
(Isa. 65. & 11:6 – 9)

SHALOM

Priests:
Give praise and
glory (worship)
to God

Rulers: 'stewarding' / 'reigning'
over creation (Rev. 22.5)

**Redeemed
Humanity**

things that God loves. God's love for the whole of his creation there-fore demands punishment for that sin. His righteousness is a direct result of his identity as a God who is love (1 John 4). All of us will be judged, and those who have not received God's forgiveness through Christ for their sin will not be included in that final kingdom, but will be cast out of God's presence.

There are a number of passages that talk about this, and despite these, the criteria we will be judged by sometimes come as a surprise to us. Revelation 11:18 says, "The time has come... for destroying those who destroy the earth." In Matthew 25: 31-46, Jesus talks directly about judgment and uses an illustration of a shepherd separating the sheep from the goats. The criteria by which they are separated and will be judged is very clear; those who have looked after the needs of the poor and vulnerable will enter God's kingdom, and those that have ignored them will be thrown out of God's presence.

> The cross is wholly adequate for our salvation, and faith in Jesus is the only source of salvation. We are therefore not saved by good works, but we are certainly saved for good works

These passages are not saying that we are saved by works rather than faith. The Bible is clear that we can never match up to God's standards or appear righteous before God by our own effort. We are saved by God's grace alone, through faith in Christ Jesus. The cross is wholly adequate for our salvation, and faith in Jesus is the only source of salvation. We are therefore not saved *by* good works, but we are certainly saved *for* good works.[19] (Ephesians 2:8-10)

19 Stott, J & Wright, C. Christian Mission in the Modern World. (2015)

It is our lives and actions that demonstrate the reality of our faith, and therefore our salvation. In Matthew 7:21, Jesus says, "Not everyone who says to me, 'Lord, Lord,' will enter the kingdom of heaven, but only he who does the will of my Father who is in heaven." It is by our lives that we are identified as members of his kingdom. As James says, "I will show you my faith by what I do." (James 2:18) and, "faith without deeds is dead." (James 2:26). In 1 John we read that our love for God is demonstrated in our love for our brothers and sisters (1 John 4: 7-21). If our lives do not demonstrate the love and grace that we have received through Christ to others, then we disqualify ourselves from receiving his grace (Matthew 7:1,2) and dwelling in his presence forever.

As we live out our lives, we should be working towards the fulfillment of God's kingdom here on earth, with the source of our joy and hope being the knowledge that when Christ returns, God's kingdom will be fully established and will last for ever and ever, for his eternal glory.

Key points:

- The new heavens and new earth /new Jerusalem as the final phase of God's plan

- The new heavens and the new earth as our final resting place (not heaven) where God once again lives with humanity and all the relationships broken at the fall are restored

- Our role is to build God's kingdom here on earth as we wait expectantly for his final return

- Judgement as the inevitable consequence of sin, because sin harms that which God loves - humanity and all the rest of creation.

- The hope that we have as believers is the assurance of God's final victory and the establishment of his eternal Kingdom. This is a story with a beginning and an ending

Conclusions

THE bible story tells us 'who we are, where we have come from, how we got to be here, why the world is in the mess it is in, how it can be (and has been) changed, and where we are ultimately going.'[20]

What can we conclude from our overview of the biblical story? We see through the whole diversity of the 66 books of the Bible, God's character of love and justice and his mission to restore through Christ all the relationships broken at the fall, thereby reconciling to himself all things. The 'holistic mess' that occurred through the fall needs a holistic or integral solution to it –

> The 'holistic mess' that occurred through the fall needs a holistic or integral solution to it – and God's redemptive plan, through Jesus, is definitely that.

and God's redemptive plan, through Jesus, is definitely that.[21] God's mission is holistic, or integral, by nature and definition. God's passion and concern for justice is clearly demonstrated in his actions through the way he has acted in history, through the law, and through the life and teaching of Jesus. The grace he has shown to us we must show to others.

We are called to be a part of that integral or holistic plan, for the redemption of the whole of creation; living our lives as ambassadors of Christ, as salt and light in society, discipling nations, through the whole of our lives - who we are, what we do and what we say.

Does that mean that there is only one way to do mission? Is there a cer-

20 C. Wright. The Mission of God. (IVP, 2006)
21 Ibid

tain proportion of our resources that we should dedicate to each aspect of mission? Do we need to get the balance right if we are to claim to be doing 'integral mission'?

> ...as the church we are all called to live as people made in the image of God, as members of His Kingdom; reflecting His character; engaged in His mission; and living in prophetic expectation of the fulfillment of His Kingdom.

God makes us different, with different skills and different callings – both as individuals and as organisations. We need to be faithful to our calling. But as the church we are all called to live as people made in the image of God, as members of his kingdom; reflecting his character; engaged in his mission; and living in prophetic expectation of the fulfillment of his kingdom. The Gospel should impact on all aspects of our lives.

In 1 John 2: 5,6 we are told that, "Whoever claims to live in him, must walk as Jesus did." The challenge we need to ask ourselves is: are we walking as Jesus did?

I would like to end by quoting, with a few minor amendments, the climactic conclusion of Chris Wright's book The Mission of God[22]:

"This biblical story challenges our self-centred worldview (ego-centrism):

We ask "where does God fit into the story of my life" when we should ask "where does my little life fit into the great story of God?"

We ask "what is my individual purpose?" when we should be seeing the purpose of all life, including our own, in the mission of God.

We talk about the challenge of "applying the Bible to our lives" when the

22 Wright, C. J. H. The Mission of God (2006)

real question is, "How do I apply my life to the Bible?"

We wrestle with how to make the gospel relevant to the World, when the reality is that God is transforming the world to fit the reality and shape of the Gospel.

We wonder, for example, whether creation care might fit into our concept and practice of mission, when this story challenges us to ask ,"Are our lives aligned with God's mission or not?"

We argue as to what can legitimately be included in the mission God expects from our church, when we should be asking, "What kind of church does God expect for his mission?"

I may wonder what kind of mission God has for me – when I should ask, "What kind of me does God want for his mission?"

Bibliography and Further Reading

Bartholomew, C & Goheen, M. The Drama of Scripture. Finding our place in the Biblical story (Baker Academic, 2006).

Bookless, D. Planetwise: Dare to care for God's world (Intervarsity Press, 2008)

Jacoby, D A. A Quick Overview of the Bible. Understanding how all the pieces fit together (Harvest House Publishers, 2012)

Pawson, D. Unlocking the Bible. A unique overview of the whole Bible (Harper Collins, 2007)

Reimer, J. Missio Politica: The Mission of Church and Politics (Langham Global Library, 2017)

Roberts, V. God's Big Picture: Tracing the Storyline of the Bible (Intervarsity press, 2002)

Stott, J. Christian Mission in the Modern World. Updated and expanded by Chris Wright (Intervarsity Press, 2015)

Wright, C J H. Old Testament Ethics for the People of God (Intervarsity Press, 2004)

Wright, C J H. The Mission of God: Unlocking the Bible's Grand Narrative (Intervarsity press, 2006)

Wright, C J H. The Mission of God's people: A Biblical Theology of the Church's Mission (Zondervan, 2010)

Wright, T. Surprised by Hope (SPCK, 2007)

 **micah**

MICAH Global is a world-wide movement of Christian organisations, institutions and individuals networking and acting together towards a transforming and integral mission that sees the church as an agent of change in every community.

We are a catalyst, a movement and a network for transforming mission with a special focus on mobilising a united response towards reducing poverty, addressing injustice and enabling reconciliation and conflict resolution around the world.

We work to deepen the understanding and application of integral mission as expressed through ministry responses such as relief, rehabilitation, development, creation care, justice, and peace-making and reconciliation initiatives.

Established in 2001, Micah now has over 800 members in 93 countries. Our vision inspires us towards the realisation of communities living life in all its fullness, free from extreme poverty, injustice or conflict.

> Micah Global's motivating call to action is expressed in Micah 6:8. "What does the Lord require of you? To act justly and to love mercy, and to walk humbly with your God."

Connect with us www.micahglobal.org

Lightning Source UK Ltd.
Milton Keynes UK
UKHW020616070619
343999UK00007B/1012/P